Sports Illustrated KIDS

W9-CBA-678

BASKETBALL STATS
AND THE STORIES BEHIND THEM

What Every Fan Needs to Know

by Eric Braun

CAPSTONE PRESS
a capstone imprint

Sports Illustrated Kids Stats & Stories are published by Capstone Press,
1710 Roe Crest Drive, North Mankato, Minnesota 56003.
www.mycapstone.com

Library of Congress Cataloging-in-Publication Data
Names: Braun, Eric, 1971– author.
Title: Basketball stats and the stories behind them : what every fan needs to know /
by Eric Braun.
Description: North Mankato, Minnesota : Capstone Press, 2016. | Series:
Sports Illustrated Kids. Sports Stats and Stories. | Includes
bibliographical references, webography and index.
Identifiers: LCCN 2015039017| ISBN 9781491482162 (Library Binding) | ISBN
9781491485859 (Paperback) | ISBN 9781491485897 (eBook PDF)
Subjects: LCSH: Basketball players—Statistics—Juvenile literature.
Basketball—History—Juvenile literature.
Classification: LCC GV885.1 .B73 2016 | DDC 796.323021—dc23
LC record available at http://lccn.loc.gov/2015039017

Editorial Credits
Nick Healy, editor; Ted Williams, designer; Eric Gohl, media researcher;
Tori Abraham, production specialist

Photo Credits
Getty Images: Sports Illustrated/Dick Raphael, 30; Sports Illustrated: Al Tielemans,
13, 23, Andy Hayt, 5, 10, 44, Bill Frakes, 15, 26, David E. Klutho, 20, 33, John G.
Zimmerman, 8, John Iacono, 27, John W. McDonough, 6, 7, 14, 16, 19, 21, 24, 29, 36,
37, 39, 41 (all), 43 (right), Manny Millan, 35, 45 (bottom), Richard Meek, 34, Robert
Beck, 12, 25, 43 (left), 45 (top), Simon Bruty, cover, 1

Editor's Note:
All statistics are through the 2014–15 NBA season unless otherwise noted.

Printed in the United States of America in North Mankato, Minnesota.
032019   000068

TABLE OF CONTENTS

STATS ON THE COURT

On April 16, 1987, the second-to-last game of the season, Michael Jordan and the Chicago Bulls faced Dominique Wilkins and the Atlanta Hawks. The game provided a matchup between two of basketball's brightest stars, but it was Jordan who stole the show. He put up 61 points, giving him more than 3,000 that season. Previously only the legendary Wilt Chamberlain had surpassed the 3,000-points mark in a single season.

Jordan's 61 that night was a signature performance in an amazing season. He had averaged 37.1 points per game. He scored 40 or more points 37 times and 50 or more 8 times. He won the scoring title, beginning a run of seven scoring titles in a row.

If you weren't alive to witness Jordan back then, you can still easily understand how well he played by looking at his points per game, steals, and other statistics. If you did get to see him, stats are a fun way to relive the games. Numbers tell stories.

Sportswriters use statistics to describe completed games and to preview upcoming contests. Players, coaches, and team executives use stats, too. Numbers can help them decide which players should be on the floor. Numbers also help them understand which players are best in certain situations or in specific parts of the game. In professional basketball, teams are always looking for an edge. Stats can give it to them.

Baseball was the true trailblazer in using stats. In that sport, it's easy to break down the action pitch by pitch. But basketball is fast-moving and always in motion. All 10 players on the floor influence every play. For example, a possession might end in a blocked shot, but "blocked shot" in the box score doesn't tell the whole story. It doesn't tell, for instance, about the botched screen that led to a bad pass that led to the ill-advised shot. It doesn't tell about the fierce defense off the ball.

Certainly statistics are imperfect, but they are also useful and constantly improving. Sportswriters, coaches, fans, and analysts are always looking for new and better ways to use numbers to understand what happens on the hardwood. Stats help explain the game they love.

CHAPTER 1

Who are your favorite National Basketball Association (NBA) stars? If you're like most fans, you probably love the guys who put up big points. Maybe you follow LeBron James, Kevin Durant, Stephen Curry, Carmelo Anthony, and Kobe Bryant. Or maybe you're into legends like Michael Jordan, Larry Bird, Magic Johnson, and Dr. J.

These current and past players rank as some of the game's greats. They are stars and legends for many reasons, but scoring is perhaps the main reason. Basketball superstars are the players who score big game after game, season after season.

Many people consider Michael Jordan to be the best NBA player of all time. But in many ways, the sport has never had a bigger star than Wilt Chamberlain. Not only did he score 100 points in a single game, he had one season, 1961–62, during which he averaged 50.4 points per game. Think of that, 50 points on an average night.

▶ JAMES HARDEN

WHY AVERAGE MATTERS

Any player can have a good game. It takes a special player to score big points on a regular basis. Figuring a player's points per game (PPG) provides a picture of his ability to fill up the bucket—and keep filling it.

Simply add up all the points a player scores over a certain period, and then divide by the number of games he played. For example, in the 2014–15 season, Houston Rockets guard James Harden scored an eye-popping 2,217 points. He played in 81 games. (An NBA season has 82 games, and Harden missed one. Stats that look at averages, like PPG, ignore games in which a player doesn't play.)

2,217 ÷ 81 = 27.4 PPG

Harden's 27.4 PPG was good for second-best in the league for 2014–15. He trailed only Russell Westbrook of the Oklahoma Thunder.

PPG LEADERS, 2014–15

Rank	Player	Team	PPG
1.	RUSSELL WESTBROOK	THUNDER	28.1
2.	JAMES HARDEN	ROCKETS	27.4
3.	LEBRON JAMES	CAVALIERS	25.3
4.	ANTHONY DAVIS	PELICANS	24.4
5.	DEMARCUS COUSINS	KINGS	24.1
6.	STEPHEN CURRY	WARRIORS	23.8
7.	LAMARCUS ALDRIDGE	TRAILBLAZERS	23.4
8.	BLAKE GRIFFIN	CLIPPERS	21.9
9.	KYRIE IRVING	CAVALIERS	21.7
	KLAY THOMPSON	WARRIORS	21.7

▲ RUSSELL WESTBROOK

Was Wilt a greater scorer than Jordan? He had several seasons that were better than Jordan's best, but over their careers, Jordan edged Wilt in PPG. They rank first and second on the top-five list, which is rounded out by two players who are active today— LeBron James and Kevin Durant.

▼ WILT CHAMBERLAIN

PPG, CAREER LEADERS

Rank	Player	Team	PPG
1.	MICHAEL JORDAN	BULLS/WIZARDS	30.12
2.	WILT CHAMBERLAIN	WARRIORS/76ERS/LAKERS	30.07
3.	ELGIN BAYLOR	LAKERS	27.36
4.	LEBRON JAMES*	CAVALIERS/HEAT	27.35
5.	KEVIN DURANT*	SUPERSONICS/THUNDER	27.31

* active player

POSTSEASON STARS

Scoring loads of points during the regular season is important, but legends are made in the playoffs. In the intense pressure of postseason play, Jordan was better than any player before or since his time.

PLAYOFF PPG, CAREER LEADERS

Rank	Player	Team	PPG
1.	MICHAEL JORDAN	BULLS/WIZARDS	33.5
2.	ALLEN IVERSON	76ERS/NUGGETS/PISTONS/GRIZZLIES	29.7
3.	JERRY WEST	LAKERS	29.1
4.	KEVIN DURANT*	SUPERSONICS/THUNDER	28.9
5.	LEBRON JAMES*	CAVALIERS/HEAT	28.0

* active player

SPEAKING OF BIG GAMES

Sometimes a player has a special game, like when Michael Jordan scored 69 points against the Cleveland Cavaliers in 1990 or when Kobe Bryant dropped 81 on the Toronto Raptors in 2006. But the granddaddy of all big games belongs to Wilt Chamberlain. On March 2, 1962, he scored an even 100 points against the New York Knicks. In the record game, Wilt made 28 free throws and scored 72 points from the field. His Philadelphia Warriors won 169–147.

CHAPTER 2

When you think about what makes a hoops powerhouse, do you think about teams that score a lot of points? The 1981–82 Denver Nuggets averaged 126.5 points per game, the highest team total in NBA history. Three Nuggets averaged more than 20 PPG. Kiki Vandeweghe led the team in shooting percentage while trailing Alex English and Dan Issel in points scored.

But the Nuggets didn't seriously challenge for the title that season. They took second in their division and lost in the first round of the playoffs. The L.A. Lakers had been second in team PPG during the regular season, and they went on to win the NBA Championship.

▶ KIKI VANDEWEGHE

CALCULATING PPG

To figure out PPG for a season, add up all the points a team scored in the season and divide it by 82 (the number of games in a season). The 1981–82 Nuggets scored 10,371 points.

10,371 ÷ 82 = 126.5

Team PPG is a blunt way to measure a team's offensive firepower.

TOP SCORING TEAMS OF ALL TIME

The greatest teams in NBA history—such as the Minneapolis Lakers of the 1950s, the Boston Celtics of the 1960s, the L.A. Lakers and Celtics of the 1980s, and the Chicago Bulls of the 1990s—don't make the list of the highest scoring teams of all time.

Rules changes and other factors have changed the game over time. A quick look at the all-time leaders shows that the 1960s and 1980s were high-scoring eras. The modern game became more defensive, although in recent years scoring has been on the rise again.

TEAM PPG, ALL-TIME LEADERS

Rank	Season	Team	PPG	W-L
1.	1981–82	NUGGETS	126.5	46–36
2.	1961–62	WARRIORS	125.4	49–31
3.	1966–67	76ERS	125.2	68–13
4.	1959–60	CELTICS	124.5	59–16
5.	1983–84	NUGGETS	123.7	38–44
6.	1982–83	NUGGETS	123.2	45–37
7.	1961–62	ROYALS	123.1	43–37
8.	1967–68	76ERS	122.6	62–20
9.	1966–67	WARRIORS	122.4	44–37
10.	1969–70	76ERS	121.9	42–40

By measuring PPG against how many points a team gives up, you can see a fuller picture of the team.

For example, consider this tale of two L.A. teams from 2013–14. The Clippers scored the league-high PPG with 107.9 and gave up 101.0, for a differential of +6.9. The Lakers, meanwhile, scored 103.0 PPG, but they gave up 109.2, for a differential of -6.2.

That's why the Clippers finished 57–25 and won their division while the Lakers finished 27–55 and finished 35 games out of first place.

In 2014–15 the team with the best differential was the Warriors, who won the championship. The worst team was the Knicks.

▶ BLAKE GRIFFIN, CLIPPERS

▶ KLAY THOMPSON, WARRIORS

TEAM SCORING DIFFERENTIAL LEADERS, 2014–15

Rank	Team	Points For	Points Against	Differential
1.	WARRIORS	110.0	99.9	+10.1
2.	CLIPPERS	106.7	100.1	+6.6
3.	SPURS	103.2	97.0	+6.2
4.	HAWKS	102.5	97.1	+5.4
5.	CAVALIERS	103.1	98.7	+4.4

CHAPTER 3

FIELD GOAL PERCENTAGE

▶ DEANDRE JORDAN

Some players score lots of points because they get lots of minutes and they take lots of shots. They might miss a lot, but because they take so many shots they end up with lots of points. Total points and points per game don't tell us how good of a shooter someone is.

What does? Field goal percentage (FG%). A player's FG% is his or her number of baskets made divided by the number of shots taken.

DeAndre Jordan has led the league in FG% for three years running. In 2014–15, he made 379 of the 534 shots he took.

379 ÷ 534 = .710

In spite of leading the league in FG%, Jordan is never anywhere near the league leaders in points. One reason for that is the position he plays. Jordan is a center, and he scores nearly all of his points in the paint. Those are close-range, easy shots. Jordan attempted only six three-pointers in his first seven years in the NBA, missing all of them. His poor free-throw shooting also keeps him off the list of league leaders in scoring.

FG% LEADERS, 2014–15

Rank	Player	Team	%
1.	DEANDRE JORDAN	CLIPPERS	.710
2.	JONAS VALANCIUNAS	RAPTORS	.572
3.	MARCIN GORTAT	WIZARDS	.567
4.	TIMOFEY MOZGOV	CAVALIERS	.555
5.	TYLER ZELLER	CELTICS	.549
6.	AL HORFORD	HAWKS	.538
7.	ANTHONY DAVIS	PELICANS	.535
8.	DERRICK FAVORS	JAZZ	.525
9.	NIKOLA VUCEVIC	MAGIC	.523
10.	ENES KANTER	THUNDER	.519

▲ MARCIN GORTAT

CHAPTER 4

THREE-POINT PERCENTAGE

An effective post player like DeAndre Jordan can be valuable to a team. That's obvious. But when they want to rack up points in a hurry, coaches look to their long-range shooters. Indeed, to explode for big points in a hurry, there's no greater weapon than the three-pointer.

The Golden State Warriors demonstrated that fact in a February 2015 game against the Dallas Mavericks. The Mavs jumped out to an early 20-point lead, and to cut into the deficit, the Warriors' Stephen Curry started launching the threes. He made 6 of 7 three-pointers in the third quarter alone and finished the game 10 of 16 from behind the arc.

$10 \div 16 = .625$ three-point percentage

Because he was so efficient with the threes, Curry ended the night with an impressive 51 points. And the Warriors stormed back to win 128–114.

▶ STEPHEN CURRY

TERRIFIC TEAMMATES

Amazingly, Curry wasn't the first player on his team to score 50 or more in one game that season. Just a couple weeks earlier, Klay Thompson scored 52 against the Sacramento Kings. That put the teammates in elite company.

TEAMMATES SCORING 50+, SINGLE SEASON

Season	Players	Team
2014–15	STEPHEN CURRY AND KLAY THOMPSON	WARRIORS
1994–95	JAMAL MASHBURN AND JIM JACKSON	MAVERICKS
1994–95	DANA BARROS AND WILLIE BURTON	76ERS
1984–85	LARRY BIRD AND KEVIN MCHALE	CELTICS
1979–80	GEORGE GERVIN AND LARRY KENON	SPURS
1961–62	BOB PETTIT AND CLIFF HAGAN	HAWKS
1961–62	JERRY WEST, ELGIN BAYLOR, AND RUDY LARUSSO	LAKERS

SHARPSHOOTING LEGEND

The most accurate three-point shooter of all time was Steve Kerr, with 45.4 percent for his career. In his playing years, Kerr won five NBA championships, including three with the Chicago Bulls and two with the San Antonio Spurs. He also won one in his first year as a head coach when he led the Golden State Warriors to the title in 2014–15. At that time one of Kerr's players, Stephen Curry, sat at number three on the all-time list of three-point leaders with a 44.4 percentage.

CHAPTER 5
EFFECTIVE FIELD GOAL PERCENTAGE

Consider two players:

Player A is a big man—over seven feet tall. He plays center and sinks lots of buckets from up close. His FG% is an impressive .555, but he attempted only six three-pointers for the year and made only two of them.

Player B does his damage from all over the floor. His FG% is much lower than that of Player A—just .436. But he attempted 457 three-pointers and made 191 of them.

Who's the more valuable shooter? If you consider only FG%, Player A looks more valuable. He was much more efficient, hitting 12 percent more of his shots.

FACTORING IN THE THREES

Player A is Timofey Mozgov of the Cleveland Cavaliers. Player B is San Antonio Spurs shooting guard, Danny Green. Does knowing their names change your mind about who's more valuable?

To get a better picture of what shooters are doing, coaches, players, and fans need a shooting percentage stat that factors in the extra points scored on three-pointers. That's what effective field goal percentage (eFG%) does. With eFG%, Green gets a big boost for all the threes he makes.

► DANNY GREEN

Here's how it works: You take the player's total field goals and add one-half of his number of three-pointers. Then you divide that number by the player's total field goal attempts:

(field goals + .5 (3-pt field goals)) ÷ field goal attempts

Green made 322 field goals and 191 three-point shots out of his total of 738 field goal attempts.

(322 + .5 (191)) ÷ 738 = .566 eFG%

In comparison, Mozgov's eFG% was .557, so Green was slightly more efficient shooting when measured this way.

Obviously, teams want to make more shots and miss fewer of them. Making shots is how you score points, and scoring points is how you win. But teams can tolerate a few more misses (and thus a lower FG%) when some of the shots made are threes (and thus a higher eFG%).

EFG% LEADERS, 2014–15

Rank	Player	Team	%
1.	DEANDRE JORDAN	CLIPPERS	.711
2.	STEPHEN CURRY	WARRIORS	.594
3.	J.J. REDICK	CLIPPERS	.583
4.	DEMARRE CARROLL	HAWKS	.579
5.	JONAS VALANCIUNAS	RAPTORS	.572

▶ DEMARRE CARROLL

◀ TYSON CHANDLER

ALL-TIME EFG% LEADERS

Rank	Player	Team	%
1.	TYSON CHANDLER*	BULLS/HORNETS/BOBCATS/ MAVERICKS/KNICKS	.5913
2.	SHAQUILLE O'NEAL	MAGIC/LAKERS/HEAT/SUNS/ CAVALIERS/CELTICS	.5823
3.	ARTIS GILMORE	COLONELS/BULLS/SPURS/CELTICS	.5820
4.	MARK WEST	MAVERICKS/BUCKS/CAVALIERS/ SUNS/PISTONS/PACERS/HAWKS	.5804
5.	DWIGHT HOWARD*	MAGIC/LAKERS/ROCKETS	.5796

* active player

CHAPTER 6

FREE THROW PERCENTAGE

It was the 2000 NBA Finals. The Indiana Pacers were facing the Los Angeles Lakers. The Pacers had lost the first game in the series, and they were desperate to find a way to slow down the Lakers' star big man, Shaquille O'Neal. Their strategy? Foul him repeatedly, sending him to the free throw line to take undefended shots.

How does that make sense?

PLAYING THE ODDS

Some players are really good at shooting from the floor but not so good at making free throws. This can lead defenders to commit more fouls against such a shooter. The defenders know that fouling to prevent an easy layup is a good move because the player likely won't sink both of his free throws.

HACK-A-SHAQ

So what was Indiana doing by giving Shaq so many free throws? It was actually a smart move, because Shaq was terrible at making free throws. His free throw percentage (FT%) was a meager .524 that year, which was lower than his FG% of .574. By fouling him, the Pacers lowered the likelihood that Shaq would get two points.

SHAQUILLE O'NEAL

To calculate FT%, divide the number of free throws made by the number of attempts. In the NBA a FT% of about .750 is average. In 1999–2000 Shaq made only 432 of 824 free throws.

432 ÷ 824 = .524

The strategy of fouling a poor free throw shooter came to be known as "Hack-a-Shaq," but it has been used on many good players over the years. Recently DeAndre Jordan has faced it. His FT% for 2014–15 was just .397.

NAILING FREE THROWS

Of course, most players shoot free throws better than DeAndre Jordan and Shaq. Here are the leaders in FT% from 2014–15. When Warriors point guard Stephen Curry was named the NBA's 2014–15 MVP, his league-best free throw shooting was no small part of the reason.

TOP FREE THROW SHOOTERS, 2014–15

▲ CHRIS PAUL

Rank	Player	Team	FT%
1.	STEPHEN CURRY	WARRIORS	.914
2.	JODIE MEEKS	PISTONS	.906
3.	J.J. REDICK	CLIPPERS	.901
	JAMAL CRAWFORD	CLIPPERS	.901
5.	CHRIS PAUL	CLIPPERS	.900
6.	DANILO GALLINARI	NUGGETS	.895
7.	NICK YOUNG	LAKERS	.892
8.	DIRK NOWITZKI	MAVERICKS	.882
9.	JARRETT JACK	NETS	.881
	KEVIN MARTIN	TIMBERWOLVES	.881

Back in 1993, Michael Williams of the Minnesota Timberwolves set a record by sinking 97 consecutive free throws without a miss. For his career, Williams shot 86.8 percent from the line—good, but not good enough to make the top ten of all time.

► STEVE NASH

TOP FREE THROW SHOOTERS, CAREER

Rank	Player	Team	FT%
1.	STEVE NASH	SUNS/MAVERICKS/LAKERS	.9043
2.	MARK PRICE	CAVALIERS/BULLETS/WARRIORS/MAGIC	.9039
3.	STEPHEN CURRY*	WARRIORS	.9000
4.	PEJA STOJAKOVIC	KINGS/PACERS/HORNETS/ RAPTORS/MAVERICKS	.8948
5.	CHAUNCEY BILLUPS	CELTICS/RAPTORS/NUGGETS/ TIMBERWOLVES/PISTONS/KNICKS/CLIPPERS	.8940
6.	RAY ALLEN*	BUCKS/SUPERSONICS/CELTICS/HEAT	.8939
7.	RICK BARRY	WARRIORS/OAKS/CAPITOLS/ NETS/WARRIORS/ROCKETS	.8931
8.	CALVIN MURPHY	ROCKETS	.8916
9.	SCOTT SKILES	BUCKS/PACERS/MAGIC/BULLETS/76ERS	.8891
10.	REGGIE MILLER	PACERS	.8877

* active player

OLD-SCHOOL SHOOTER

Rick Barry, the seventh all-time leader in FT%, had an unusual way of shooting free throws—he shot underhand, also known as granny style. Barry taught his teammate George Johnson, a center, to shoot granny style, too. Johnson raised his FT% by more than 20 percent.

CHAPTER 7

BLOCKS AND STEALS

These are the flashy stats of defense. Nothing is more impressive than seeing a defender swat away an attempted shot or intercept a pass and dash off on a fast-break.

Perhaps the most fearsome shot-blocker of all time was 7-foot-2 center Dikembe Mutombo, who would wag his long finger after every block as if to say, "Not in my house!" Over his 18 years in the NBA, Mutombo blocked 3,289 shots. That's more than anyone in the league's history except the Rockets' Hakeem Olajuwon, who swatted 3,830 and won two titles in Houston.

Among active players, Anthony "The Brow" Davis of the New Orleans Pelicans is a feared shot-blocker. In 2014–15, he led the league in that category, ending Serge Ibaka's four-season run as the blocks king.

TOP SHOT-BLOCKERS, 2014–15

Rank	Player	Team	Shots Blocked
1.	ANTHONY DAVIS	PELICANS	200
2.	RUDY GOBERT	JAZZ	189
3.	DEANDRE JORDAN	CLIPPERS	183
4.	SERGE IBAKA	THUNDER	155
5.	ANDRE DRUMMOND	PISTONS	153

◀ ANTHONY DAVIS

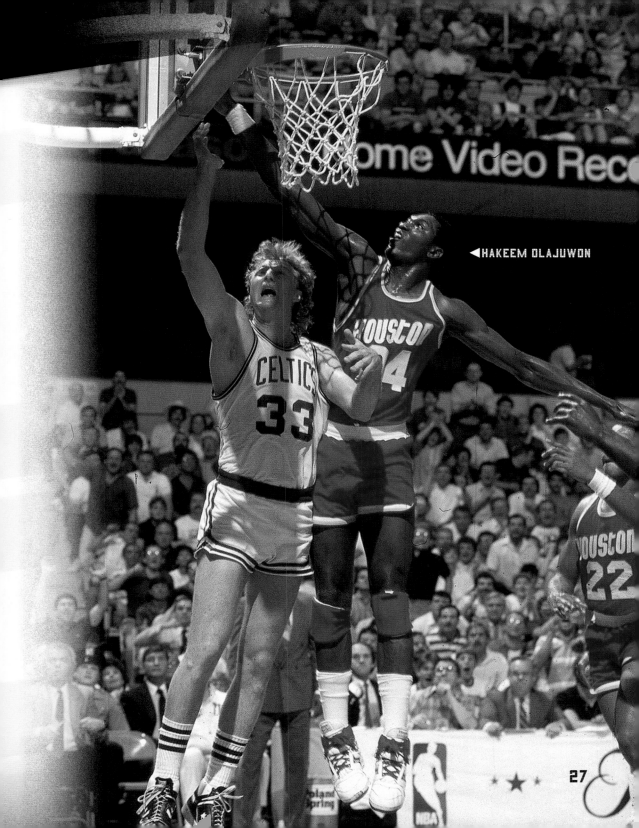

◀HAKEEM OLAJUWON

27

THIEVES ON THE HARD COURT

Blocks and steals have always been an important part of the game, but the NBA didn't start tracking them as stats until the 1973–74 season. Chris Paul of the L.A. Clippers is one of today's best at stealing. Paul led the league for four years in a row in steals per game (SPG) and remained top five in 2014–15.

To figure out steals per game, simply divide the player's total number of steals by the number of games he played.

STEALS PER GAME LEADERS, 2014–15

Rank	Player	Team	GP	STL	SPG
1.	KAWHI LEONARD	SPURS	64	148	2.31
2.	RUSSELL WESTBROOK	THUNDER	67	140	2.09
3.	TONY ALLEN	GRIZZLIES	63	129	2.05
4.	STEPHEN CURRY	WARRIORS	80	163	2.04
5.	CHRIS PAUL	CLIPPERS	82	156	1.90
	JAMES HARDEN	ROCKETS	81	154	1.90

GAMBLING ON DEFENSE

There is a downside to blocks and steals, as they both mean taking a chance. If you try for a steal or block and don't get it, you usually end up out of position. You can't defend the player, and your opponent has an open shot.

◄ KAWHI LEONARD

CHAPTER 8

ASSISTS

If you love basketball and follow the game, you will someday see the highlight. It's a famous play, and the video clip of it gets replayed dozens of times every season. In it, Celtics star Larry Bird steals an inbounds pass in the waning seconds of a 1987 playoff game against the Pistons. The play is known as "Bird's steal," but what he did next made it legendary.

LARRY BIRD ▼

After tipping away the pass lofted by Pistons guard Isiah Thomas, Bird grabbed the ball at the baseline, turned, and snapped a pass to a teammate streaking toward the hoop. That teammate, Dennis Johnson, drained a layup to give the Celtics a one-point lead with one second left on the clock. Bird's assist was every bit as important as his steal, of course.

An assist is a pass that directly sets up a basket. Fans roar for players who make awesome assists. Sometimes it's a sneaky behind-the-back pass, and sometimes it's a bounce pass in traffic. Sometimes it's a court-length bomb. In Bird's case, it was a chest pass from short range, but it was a crucial assist.

Setting up a teammate to score takes vision and accuracy. Game in and game out, teams look to their point guards to lead them on the court and to run the offense. While some point guards also put up big points, their main job is to distribute the ball.

ASSIST LEADERS, 2014–15

Rank	Player	Team	GP	AST	APG
1.	CHRIS PAUL	CLIPPERS	82	838	10.2
2.	JOHN WALL	WIZARDS	79	792	10.0
3.	TY LAWSON	NUGGETS	75	720	9.6
4.	RUSSELL WESTBROOK	THUNDER	67	574	8.6
5.	RAJON RONDO	CELTICS/MAVERICKS	68	538	7.9

THE PINCH DISHER

In February 2015 the Philadelphia 76ers found themselves in desperate need of a point guard. Their starter, Michael Carter-Williams, was injured, and days earlier the team had released his backup. They called up Tim Frazier from the developmental league. Frazier drove down from Maine, put on a Sixers uniform, and played 34 minutes in his first-ever NBA game. The previously unknown rookie dished 11 assists. The rest of his team had 11 altogether.

ASSIST TO TURNOVER RATIO

Assist to turnover ratio (AST/TO) measures a player's overall ballhandling. A player who distributes the ball and gets assists without turning the ball over will have a better ratio. A player who turns the ball over more than he gets assists will have a worse ratio. The ratio tells us who helps his teammates the most (with assists) and hurts his team the least (with turnovers).

There are plenty of ways to lose possession and therefore be charged with a turnover:

- **an opponent steals the ball**

- **an opponent intercepts a pass**

- **the player throws the ball out of bounds or steps out of bounds**

- **the player breaks a rule such as by traveling, palming, double-dribbling, committing a backcourt violation, or committing an offensive foul**

To figure out a player's AST/TO, divide the total number of assists a player has recorded in a game by the number of turnovers the player has committed in the same game. It can also be calculated over longer periods, such as a season or career.

▶ MATTHEW DELLAVEDOVA

ASSIST TO TURNOVER LEADERS, 2014–15

Rank	Player	Team	Games	AST	TO	AST/TO
1.	CHRIS PAUL	CLIPPERS	82	838	190	4.41
2.	TY LAWSON	NUGGETS	75	720	185	3.89
3.	J.J. BAREA	MAVERICKS	77	263	70	3.76
4.	MATTHEW DELLAVEDOVA	CAVALIERS	67	204	61	3.34
5.	GEORGE HILL	PACERS	43	220	69	3.19
6.	KEMBA WALKER	HORNETS	62	318	100	3.18
7.	BRANDON JENNINGS	PISTONS	41	272	90	3.02
8.	JRUE HOLIDAY	PELICANS	40	274	91	3.01
9.	DERON WILLIAMS	NETS	68	448	154	2.91
10.	DEVIN HARRIS	MAVERICKS	76	237	85	2.79

▶ BILL RUSSELL

34

We all know that the NBA stars who get the most attention are the ones who score the most points. But what happens when those shots don't go in? Someone has to be there to clean up. In other words, someone needs to get the rebound. Rebounds are of critical importance in every game.

Some players have built careers around being rebound machines. Dennis Rodman was never a great scorer. But "Rodzilla" was a monster on the boards, leading the league in rebounds per game (RPG) for seven consecutive years.

Hall of Famer Bill Russell won 11 championships with the Boston Celtics in the 1960s. He was MVP five times, but he never finished higher than 15th in the league in scoring. One of the things that made him so valuable was his rebounding. Russell pulled down 21,620 rebounds in his career, including 53 in one game.

REBOUND KINGS
NBA Rebounding Titles

Rank	Player	Titles
1.	WILT CHAMBERLAIN	11
2.	DENNIS RODMAN	7
3.	MOSES MALONE	6
4.	DWIGHT HOWARD	5
5.	KEVIN GARNETT	4
	BILL RUSSELL	4

▲ DENNIS RODMAN

REBOUNDS PER GAME

Wilt Chamberlain holds many offensive records, but he was also a top-notch defender and rebounder. Chamberlain took the NBA rebounding title 11 times, and he still holds the record for rebounds per game, with an average of 22.9 for his career.

To calculate RPG, divide the player's total number of rebounds by the number of games played. Chamberlain pulled down 23,924 rebounds in his career and played in 1,045 games.

$$23{,}924 \div 1{,}045 = 22.89 \text{ RPG (rounded to 22.9)}$$

REBOUNDS PER GAME, CAREER

Rank	Player	Team	RPG
1.	WILT CHAMBERLAIN	WARRIORS/76ERS/LAKERS	22.9
2.	BILL RUSSELL	CELTICS	22.5
3.	BOB PETTIT	HAWKS	16.2
4.	JERRY LUCAS	ROYALS/WARRIORS/KNICKS	15.6
5.	NATE THURMOND	WARRIORS/BULLS/CAVALIERS	15.0

REBOUNDS PER GAME, 2014-15

Rank	Player	Team	RPG
1.	DEANDRE JORDAN	CLIPPERS	15.0
2.	ANDRE DRUMMOND	PISTONS	13.5
3.	DEMARCUS COUSINS	KINGS	12.7
4.	PAU GASOL	BULLS	11.8
5.	TYSON CHANDLER	MAVERICKS	11.5

▲ DEMARCUS COUSINS

◄ DEANDRE JORDAN

Soon after Shane Battier was drafted in the first round in 2001 by the Memphis Grizzlies, he might have been considered a bust. His stats were unimpressive—few points, few assists, few rebounds. He didn't lead the league in blocked shots or steals.

Somehow, though, the Grizzlies transformed quickly from the worst team in the league to a playoff team. In 2006, Battier was traded to the Houston Rockets, who had just finished 34–48. The next year Houston finished 52–30, and the year after that they went 55–27. At one point they won 22 games in a row. Many of those wins came with the Rockets' stars, Tracy McGrady and Yao Ming, out due to injuries. The one constant piece was Battier. With him on the floor, Houston simply played better.

What was going on?

MAKING THE INVISIBLE VISIBLE

What Battier was doing was invisible in traditional statistics, but it showed up clearly in plus/minus (+/-). Plus/minus looks at the difference in a team's points when a player is on the floor compared with when he's on the bench. It's a way to measure more than just a player's scoring. It measures what happens overall when he's on the court.

◄ SHANE BATTIER

39

When Battier was on the court, his teammates got better, and his opponents got worse. He didn't score an eye-popping amount of points, but the team scored more. He didn't pull down lots of rebounds, but his team did.

On defense, Battier usually guarded the NBA's leading scorers. Guess what? Battier's man typically shot worse than usual when facing him. He didn't get a bunch of steals or blocks. He just defended that player very well.

Battier's plus/minus in that first year with the Rockets was +4.5, which means his team averaged 4.5 more points over the course of a game when he played.

Plus/minus is a way to measure all the subtle things a player does to help his team play better. It can fluctuate a lot in small samples (say one or two games). Weird things can happen in a single game. But over the long haul, the stat becomes more consistent.

PLUS/MINUS LEADERS

The following tables show plus/minus in two ways—the player's total plus/minus for the season and his average plus/minus per game.

Many statisticians dislike plus/minus as a tool for evaluating players because it is so dependent on a whole team's performance. For example, a player might be doing everything very well, but if the rest of the players on the floor at the same time are not very good, his plus/minus will look bad. As the 2014–15 stats show, the players with good plus/minus scores played on two of the best teams in the NBA, while the players at the bottom of the list were on lousy teams. Andrew Wiggins won Rookie of the Year despite ranking dead last in plus/minus.

TOP FIVE IN PLUS/MINUS, 2014–15

▲ DRAYMOND GREEN

Rank	Player	Team	+/- per game	+/-
1.	STEPHEN CURRY	WARRIORS	+11.5	+920
2.	DRAYMOND GREEN	WARRIORS	+10.6	+837
3.	KLAY THOMPSON	WARRIORS	+10.1	+776
4.	CHRIS PAUL	CLIPPERS	+9.0	+735
5.	J.J. REDICK	CLIPPERS	+8.0	+626

▶ ANDREW WIGGINS

BOTTOM FIVE IN PLUS/MINUS, 2014–15

Rank	Player	Team	+/- per game	+/-
484.	SHANE LARKIN	KNICKS	-5.2	-398
485.	JASON SMITH	KNICKS	5.2	-424
486.	NERLENS NOEL	76ERS	-5.8	-432
487.	ZACH LAVINE	TIMBERWOLVES	-7.0	-540
488.	ANDREW WIGGINS	TIMBERWOLVES	-6.7	-553

CHAPTER 11

PLAYER EFFICIENCY RATING

In recent years, basketball analysts and teams have tried to do more with statistics. They know that traditional stats only tell a part of how well a player helps his team. More advanced stats like plus/minus go a little further. The player efficiency rating (PER) goes further still.

Developed by a sportswriter named John Hollinger, PER rates how productive a player is in every facet of the game. PER accounts for positive accomplishments such as field goals, free throws, three-pointers, assists, rebounds, blocks, and steals. It also looks at negative ones like missed shots, turnovers, and personal fouls. The formula for PER is extremely complicated, but basically it assigns positive point values for positive contributions and negative point values for negative contributions. Taking into account all these factors, the formula spits out a number that shows how efficient a player is per minute.

The per minute part is important. That way, players who get more minutes don't get more credit. Also, players who play fewer minutes don't get penalized. PER supplies one number that sums up everything the player does when he's on the court.

League average PER is always 15.00. Everyone starts there. If a player's PER is higher than 15.00, he is an above average player. If his PER is lower, he's below average.

2014-15 TOP FIVE IN PER
Minimum 2,000 minutes

Rank	Player	Team	PER
1.	ANTHONY DAVIS	PELICANS	30.8
2.	RUSSELL WESTBROOK	THUNDER	29.1
3.	STEPHEN CURRY	WARRIORS	28.0
4.	JAMES HARDEN	ROCKETS	26.7
5.	CHRIS PAUL	CLIPPERS	26.0

▶ ANTHONY DAVIS

▲ BEN MCLEMORE

2014-15 BOTTOM FIVE IN PER
Minimum 2,000 minutes

Player	Team	PER
WESLEY JOHNSON	LAKERS	11.1
DION WAITERS	CAVALIERS/ THUNDER	10.9
ARRON AFFLALO	BLAZERS	10.7
BEN MCLEMORE	KINGS	10.4
SOLOMON HILL	PACERS	10.21

STAT STARS

MOST POINTS SCORED, CAREER

KAREEM ABDUL-JABBAR, **38,387**

MOST MINUTES PLAYED, CAREER

KAREEM ABDUL-JABBAR, **57,446**

MOST REBOUNDS, SEASON

WILT CHAMBERLAIN, **2,149** (1960–61)

MOST REBOUNDS, CAREER

WILT CHAMBERLAIN, **23,924**

MOST POINTS, SEASON

WILT CHAMBERLAIN, **4,029** (1961–62)

HIGHEST PLAYER EFFICIENCY RATING, SEASON

WILT CHAMBERLAIN, **31.82** (1961–62)

MOST BLOCKED SHOTS, CAREER

HAKEEM OLAJUWON, **3,830**

▲ KAREEM ABDUL-JABBAR

▲ JOHN STOCKTON

MOST STEALS PER GAME, CAREER

ALVIN ROBERTSON, **2.7**

MOST ASSISTS, CAREER

JOHN STOCKTON, **15,806**

MOST STEALS, CAREER

JOHN STOCKTON, **3,265**

MOST FREE THROWS MADE, CAREER

KARL MALONE, **9,787**

MOST ASSISTS PER GAME, CAREER

MAGIC JOHNSON, **11.2**

MOST POSTSEASON POINTS, CAREER

MICHAEL JORDAN, **5,987**

▲ MAGIC JOHNSON

BEST RECORD, SINGLE SEASON

72-10, CHICAGO BULLS, 1995–96
(.8780 winning percentage)

MOST CHAMPIONSHIPS

BOSTON CELTICS, **17**

STAT GLOSSARY

assist—when a player passes to a teammate in a way that leads to a score

assist to turnover ratio—found by dividing the total number of assists a player has recorded in a game by the number of turnovers the player has committed in the same game

block—when a defender legally deflects a field goal attempt by an opponent

effective field goal percentage—a measure of shooting efficiency that accounts for the fact that a three-point field goal is worth more than a two-point field goal

field goal percentage—the ratio of field goals made to the number attempted

free throw percentage—the ratio of free throws made to the number attempted

player efficiency rating—a measure of a player's per-minute productivity; it is calculated by assigning value to all contributions a player can make, both positive and negative

plus/minus—a measure of how a player's team performs while he is on the court compared to how it performs without him

points per game, individual—the average number of points a player scores per game; it is calculated by taking all the points scored over a season, career, or other period and dividing by the number of games he played

points per game, team—the average number of points a team scores per game

rebounds—when a player gains possession of the ball after a missed shot

steal—when a defensive player legally causes a turnover

three-point percentage—the ratio of three-point shots made to the number attempted